W9-CFB-320

USBORNE

Lift-the-flap
ON THE BEACH

Alastair Smith and Laura Howell
Illustrated by Ian Jackson
Designed by Candice Whatmore and Karen Tomlins

Digital imaging by Keith Furnival

On the seashore

The seashore is where
the sea meets the land.
This seashore is a
sandy beach.

Sand is made from
tiny pieces of rock
and shells. Damp
sand is good for
making sandcastles.

Tip the bucket
over to see
what's inside.

These seagulls
are looking
for food.

This one has found
something tasty.
Lucky seagull!

Shells and pebbles

Some little seaside animals have shells.
The shells keep them safe from rough
waves and hungry birds.

The sea rubs
pebbles together
and makes
them smooth.

What's under this
empty shell?

This wood has been battered by the sea. The salty water turned it white.

Oyster shells open and close like a book.

I'm too big for this shell.

Hermit crabs live in the shells of animals that died. As they grow, they move to a bigger shell.

A rock pool

Here's a little pool in the rocks on the seashore. It's full of sea water. Little creatures live and hide in the pool.

What can you find in this rock pool?

There's lots of slimy, slippy seaweed here. Watch out when you stand on it.

These red blobs are animals called sea anemones.

The pale yellow shells are limpets.

The blue shells are mussels.

Crabs

A crab has a hard shell and two strong claws.

My claws are stronger than your hands.

Watch out! A crab can give you a nasty pinch with its claws.

Here is a fishing boat. It has caught a lot of fish.

Fish!

Fish!

The seagulls are off to grab some fish from the boat.

Fishing boats have big nets, like these. They catch lots of fish very quickly.

the rock
light shi

The light flashes
on, and off, and
on, and off...

At night
it is dark, the light
can be seen from
far, far away.

Waves batter the
land and wear it
away. This is how
the cliffs are made.

Long ago,
these rocky
stumps were
part of the cliffs.
Now look at them!

Lots of birds make their nests high up on the rocky cliffs.

These birds are gannets. They dive into the sea and grab fish to eat.

This is a puffin. She has caught some fish for her chick to eat.

Can you find the puffin's chick?

This book has shown you some of the
exciting things that you can find by the sea.
Next time you're on the beach, why not
see what else you can discover?

This new, enlarged edition first published in 2004 by Usborne Publishing Ltd, Usborne House,
83-85 Saffron Hill, London EC1N 8RT, England.
www.usborne.com
Copyright © Usborne Publishing Ltd, 2004, 2002.

The name Usborne and the devices ♛ ♈ are Trade Marks of Usborne Publishing Ltd.
All rights reserved. No part of this publication may be reproduced, stored in a
retrieval system, or transmitted in any form or by any means, electronic, mechanical, photocopying,
recording or otherwise, without the prior permission of the publisher.
UE This edition first published in America in 2004.

Printed in China.